Making Designer Furniture

Designer

for Children, the Home and Garden

Hans-Werner Bastian

Making *Designer* Furniture
for Children, the Home
and Garden

Argus Books

Contents

Making furniture with the router

The keen DIY enthusiast is capable of making attractive and practical furniture very inexpensively with some basic skills and the correct tools. An essential tool is the router and this chapter provides guidance on working techniques and tells you how to use this tool professionally.

A universal power tool

When attempting to make furniture, the do-it-yourself enthusiast cannot be without modern power tools, such as a portable circular saw, jigsaw, orbital sander or drill. Experts recognize the router as the most versatile and creative power tool. With this tool, it is possible to build superior pieces of furniture in a highly creative way. The following pages describe its use in detail.

With a router you can rebate and profile edges, make grooves, drill and cut using prepared templates. The actual tool, the cutter, sits in the chuck. The cutter is directly driven via the motor spindle at speeds of up to 27,000 RPM. With other electrically powered tools, the high speed of the universal motor must be considerably reduced via a gearbox and electronic components. With the router, however, these high speeds are highly desirable. They guarantee the best cutting results. As the professionals say: 'For clean cutting, the router must sing'. This means, that the speed must not noticeably drop under load.

A router consists of a motor and flat-bottomed framework. Cutting depth is adjusted by lowering the motor into the framework. With some devices, such as the one in the top right photo, both units are firmly connected to each other. With others, the motor can be taken out and installed for stationary work in a drill or cutting stand. Such a detachable motor can also be used as a straight grinder. Sometimes, it is even possible to install the router motor underneath saw tables, intended to accommodate stationary circular saws. It provides a table router with the same basic functions as a stationary professional machine.

With this device, motor and framework are firmly connected to each other. The cutting depth can be adjusted precisely

The router is usually guided along the material edge using a parallel fence. Grooves, for example, can be produced accurately in this way

If it is possible to remove the drive motor from the framework, the router can be equipped with an abrasive cutter and used as a straight grinder

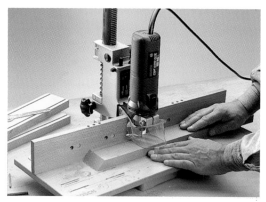

For very small pieces of work, the router must be mounted stationary and the material brought to the router

A portable tool with simple basic fittings is sufficient for occasional light duty work. The above example shows edge trimming

Cutting rule: when machining large pieces of material, the router should, whenever possible, be brought to the material; for smaller pieces, it is better to guide the material to the mounted stationary router.

The router is supplied with a straight fence for making parallel cuts. A curved fence with a roller allows working on curved edges. With the trammel point and arm, circular grooves and beads can be produced. The router is used without the guide fence for cutting embossments freehand into the surface of the wood. Sometimes, the cutter guides itself along the material edge. In this case, a ball bearing roller or guide pin below the bit runs along the edge of the board and so limits sideways movement of the router into the material.

A good router should have ergonomically shaped handles, which also allow left-handers to work without problems. It must be possible to switch on and off from the handle. Precise depth adjustment is important for the achievement of satisfactory results. High quality routers have a device for roughly pre-setting the cutting depth. After a test cut, the precision adjustment is used to correct the setting as necessary. When working with a router, always check the setting of the fence and cutting depth on a trial piece, before machining the original.

'Constant Electronic' revolution control equipment is a most useful router facility. It permits speed presetting and prevents the revolutions from dropping too much under load. It also provides, when necessary, the extra power required for maintaining the desired revolutions. The speed preselection also allows adjustment to material needs. If plastic or aluminium is machined instead of wood, lower revolutions are required.

Router cutters

Above all, the versatility of the router is due to the availability of many different types of cutters. The cutting tools are differentiated according to the different profiles they cut in wood. There are, for example, cove cutters, ovolos, bevel trimmers and many more.

Some cutters are only available for machining edges. They cannot plunge vertically into the wood because at the bottom there is no cutting edge for carrying out a boring function. Instead, such cutters are often equipped with a pin guide or even a ball bearing roller, which guides the tool along the workpiece edge.

Router cutters with a cutting underside can cut grooves of different profiles into the material surface. It is possible for them to plunge vertically into the wood and move sideways after the intended depth has been reached.

Router cutters are mainly made in two materials: the cheaper HSS material (high performance high speed steel) and the more expensive HM cutter (hardened metal, tungsten carbide tipped). Cutters with hardened cutting edges last 25 times as long as HSS cutters. They can also be used for working with chipboard and other bonded wood materials and also for aluminium and plastics. But for softwood, the best cutting result is achieved with a sharp HSS cutter.

The decision as to whether it is worthwhile buying the expensive HM cutter depends on the frequency of its use. An HM cutter which has become blunt can be resharpened by a specialist company.

On the right, some of the most important router cutters are shown. More commonly used are the **straights**. Having a diameter of 4–20 mm, they are suitable for grooves

Straight cutter

Rebate cutter

Dovetail cutter

Chamfer trimmer

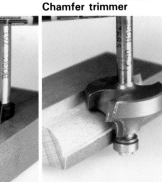
V-groove engraving

Ovolo cutter

Cove cutter

Ogee moulds

Use white spirit to clean dirty or resin soiled cutters, but do not immerse cutters with ball bearings as the bearing grease would dissolve

of different width and depth, for tenon holes and also for pre-cutting. The **dovetail cutter** is used to machine the dovetail tongue and groove joint. **V-groove and engraving bit** make the V-shaped groove required for lettering and decoration. The **cove cutter** with guide pin (photo) is used for machining edges. Without the pin, it can cut half round grooves into the surface. **Rebate cutters** are purely used for machining edges, they are available with pin or with ball bearing guide (photo). **Chamfers** with guide roller are used to bevel or chamfer material edges and **ovolos** for rounding edges. They are offered with pin or ball bearing guides. **Profile cutters** are available with different shapes. They are used, for example, for producing picture frame mouldings.

All router cutters have highly sensitive bits and must be treated with great care so that they stay sharp as long as possible.

In order to avoid damage, it is recommended that cutters are stored in a self-made stand. Depending on shank diameter, 6 or 8 mm bore holes will be required

Machining straight edges

The router is used mostly for working on workpiece edges. In most cases, the straight fence, which is part of the basic equipment, is used. As a rule, it is connected to the router base plate by two metal bars and can be moved without stepping. Fixing screws ensure that it is locked fast in the required position.

It is best to test on waste wood how far the router should cut sideways into the workpiece. Optimum cutting results are achieved with correct revolutions and shallow cuts, 1–2 mm at a time. Deep cuts should be made by a series of shallow cuts.

At the start of the operation, the straight fence lies flat against the workpiece with only half of its total width. When plunging the cutter, the fence can easily tilt by some millimetres, and the cutter will plunge too much. In this case, a corrective measure is a fence extension – a hardwood strip made by yourself, which is screwed to the actual fence.

Cutters with guide pin or ball bearing guide roller (see page 9) guarantee absolute precision when working on material edges. By using these, the sideways plunging by the cutter is automatically restricted. Of course, the material removing capability of the cutter cannot be exceeded.

It is almost impossible to exactly guide the router on especially small workpieces or narrow strips, as the fence and baseplate do not have sufficient support. In this case, the router is used stationary mounted in a drill and router stand. Take care to move in the correct direction. Always cut against the rotation of the cutter, so that the tool cuts cleanly into the wood.

It is best to use a cutter with guide pin or guide roller to cut an evenly wide rebate into a workpiece edge

Narrow parts, giving little supporting surface, are best worked on with the machine fixed in a stand

The stationary mounted router also provides its worth when grooving strips. The adjustable stand fence serves as guide

The plywood template screwed to the workpiece allows series cutting of dowel holes at equal intervals

The width of the board can be increased in this way. The loose tongue provides a large gluing area and guarantees highest strength

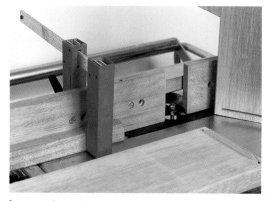

Loose plywood tongues are also used to join carcass parts of wardrobes and boxes

Woodworking joints

When constructing furniture from solid wood, joints must frequently be made. From relatively simple lap joints to dovetailed tenons, traditional carpentry techniques use many different methods. Most of these joints can be made very well and extremely precisely with the aid of a router. How much stress can be applied to a joint depends on how well the parts are interlinked and how much mating surface there is for gluing. With a lap joint, for example, half the thickness of the wood is cut away from both parts to be joined and then fixed with glue. The router, equipped with a rebate cutter (see page 9), will perform this work quicker and more exactly than could be done in the traditional way with hand tools such as tenon saw and chisel.

It is particularly easy to make dowelled joints by using a template made from plywood and the router. If working in the conventional way with a drill — without a drill stand — it is always a problem to drill the dowel holes vertically and in exactly the marked position. The router, however, with its wide baseplate provides a secure support. As a guide for precise identical cuts, a template is made from 8 mm plywood, as seen in the top left photo. Drill a 12 mm hole for each dowel. Further 4 mm bore holes serve to fix the template with chipboard screws to the workpiece. After fixing the template, equip the router with a template guide housing of 12 mm outer diameter. This insert consists of a sleeve which projects over the router baseplate and the appropriate straight cutter works within the sleeve (see also pages 9 and 17). The sleeve is put into the prepared template holes. This fixes the router exactly in the planned position. The only thing to be done is to release the router locking mechanism and to run a 6 or 8 mm straight cutter into the workpiece until the planned depth is reached. In this way, one dowel hole after the other is cut. The template can be used for the surface and also for the edge of parts to be joined. Later on, the chipboard screw holes cannot be seen — they lie covered within the joint.

Instead of using dowels, wooden parts can also be joined with loose tongue joints. As shown in the middle photo left, they enable a board's width to be increased. For this technique, the stationary mounted router equipped with a disc groove cutter goes into action. Especially demanding to make is the tongue and groove joint as shown on the top right. The correspondingly bevelled face of the mating piece is inserted into a dovetail groove. Both parts are machined with a dovetail bit.

Strong frame constructions are often needed when building furniture. Traditionally, a mortise-and-tenon joint is chosen for this. The joint is also easily made with the router, as both lower photos demonstrate. For this, the machine must be stationary mounted. The mortise is cut into the wood with a straight cutter of corresponding diameter to the tenon, which should roughly be one third of the material thickness. It is best to take a number of shallow cuts to avoid overloading the cutter. The matching tenon is cut with a rebate cutter. Before assembly, its long edges must be carefully rounded with rasp and abrasive paper. There should be a slight clearance between mortise and tenon to allow some space for the glue. With special metal templates one can also produce through-dovetail joints in series, e.g. for drawers.

If a joint must withstand tensile load, a dovetailed housing joint presents the ideal solution

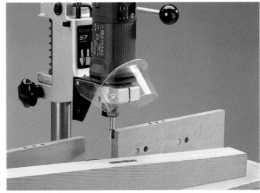

The mortise-and-tenon joint is ideal for strong frame construction. The mortise is made with a straight cutter of matching size to the tenon

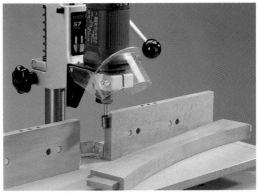

The required tenon is machined with a rebate cutter in the face of the mating part. Round the edges with a rasp

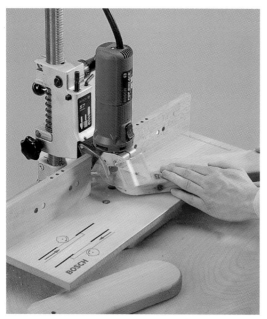

In this photo, the edge of a semicircular board end is evenly rounded by an ovolo cutter with guide pin

Machining curved edges

The straight fence cannot be used when edges of curved workpieces are to be rebated, grooved or profiled. There are guide rollers, which can be mounted underneath the baseplate and should provide a constant distance between edge and tool during cutting – but this kind of guide is not very precise. It is necessary to continuously try by eye to keep the axis between the guide roller and cutter symmetrical to the curved edge.

Only the use of cutters with guide pins or ball bearing guide rollers guarantees a really uniform cutting finish. But with these tools, the distance to the edge is fixed by the cutter dimensions. Only the depth may be varied. As the pin or roller feels every unevenness, the edge must be carefully smoothed before cutting.

When dealing with large parts, the router is always brought to the workpiece. The guide pin mounted to the ovolo feels the edge. Cut swiftly to avoid burn marks

Cutting into the material surface

How is the router moved when cutting into the surface? Use the straight edge if grooves or distinctive lines run parallel to the workpiece outer edge. In case the gap to the edge is too large or the cut does not run parallel, a strip or board can be clamped on as temporary fence and the router baseplate guided along this.

For making curved cuts into the surface, use a plywood template, at the edge of which the router equipped with a template guide housing will find a stop (see pages 16–17). The circular guide, part of the standard accessories, is available for all circular cutting operations. Just use the straight edge the other way round, so that the fence edge points upwards, and install the centring pin pointing downwards. By shifting the straight fence guide bars, different radiuses can be set. Round cuts of any size are possible if the guide bars are exchanged against longer bars of the same diameter. Decorative grooves and profiles can be made with the aid of the circular guide.

A circular cut out results from cutting with a straight cutter through the full material thickness so appropriate openings and holes can be made. Using the same technique, large wooden discs can more cleanly be cut than would be possible with a jigsaw.

Very decorative ornaments are created by combining circles and segments, as the above photo shows. Here, the individual fantasy has no limits.

Finally, lettering and reliefs can be cut into the wood. Guide the router freehand – some practise is required, because you must work without a fixed depth stop.

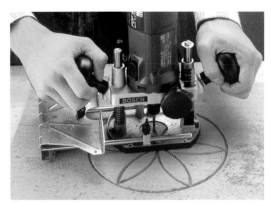

With help of the router, a decorative ornament is created from a circle and several symmetrically arranged sections

A semicircular opening is made by cutting a groove through the material using the circular guide and/or a straight fence

The skill of freehand cutting: when cutting a relief, it is necessary to guide the router and vary the depth at the same time

Template guide sleeves are available in different diameters, to match the relevant cutter. They are either screwed or pushed on

Routing with templates

In all cases, when curved lines must be cut several times and very cleanly out of a board, the router guided along a template is superior to any other tool. For this technique, the most important accessory is the template guide sleeve, which is fixed to the baseplate. It projects from the baseplate and serves as a guide for the straight cutter, which sits in the sleeve and sticks out of it. The template, made from plywood, forms the stop for the sleeve.

The illustration top right shows the arrangement of the template guide sleeve, template and cutter drawn in section. It can be seen that the cutter, running through the sleeve, always follows the template edge at a predetermined distance. This distance, which must be taken into account when making the template, is calculated to the equation:

The prepared template lies on top. Now, the router equipped with template guide sleeve and straight cutter is moved along the template edge. Following the contour, the required form is cut out

outer sleeve diameter minus cutter diameter divided by two. Cramp the prepared template to your workpiece and move the router along its edge (large photo). If the cramps get in the way, double-sided adhesive tape may be used to fasten the template. If the template lies on the workpiece underside, thin screws may be used if necessary. To reduce the load on the router and to take care of the precious tool, it is recommended that you cut large pieces with a jigsaw first, before the router is used, by sawing in the waste-wood, a few millimetres outside the intended cutting edge. Templates can also be helpful when doing delicate work. For example, for cleanly fitting butt or concealed hinges. The photo to the right shows such an application.

A further way to cut using templates is possible with the aid of a drill and router stand. For this, cut with the mounted router a 6 mm hole into the baseplate and inset into this a 6 mm metal pin (for example aluminium), which sticks out by about 5 mm. This template pin is situated exactly below the motor spindle centre. For this technique, the template is a piece of wood, into which guide grooves for the template pin are cut using the same 6 mm straight cutter. If the template is now turned over and the template pin is put onto the template, the template can be moved along on the pin.

Finally, stick the workpiece onto the template using double-sided adhesive tape. If the router, equipped with any cutter, is then lowered, it will plunge into the workpiece. Now, workpiece and template are moved along the guide groove, until the groove on the template underside has been copied on the workpiece upper side. With this method, for example, a series of drawer fronts can be decorated.

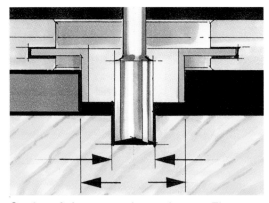

Section of sleeve, template and cutter. The cutter follows the template contour at the preset distance, which must be observed

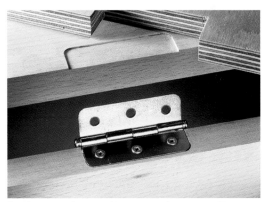

Such a template and router makes exact fitting of hinges easy. The template can be used again and again

A circular template for fitting a concealed hinge. With such aids, possible applications of the router are multiplied

Before inserting the cutter into the chuck, make sure that it has the correct shank diameter

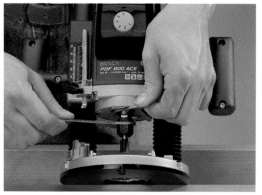

Insert the cutter shank by at least 20 mm. Motor spindle must be locked and collet chuck screw cap tightened

With this device, the template guide can be exchanged without a tool. It is secured by a bayonet fixing

Changing the tool

Routers for the home DIY enthusiast are mostly equipped with 6 or 8 mm collet chucks. Only cutters with corresponding shank diameters must be used. Forcing incorrectly sized cutter shanks to the chuck damages the high quality tool. But collet chucks can be exchanged without any problem to make possible the use of cutters of different shank diameters.

For safety reasons, always take out the plug before changing the tool. To loosen the collet chucks, lock the motor spindle and loosen the collet screw cap using a spanner. How to lock the motor spindle into position depends on the machine type. Sometimes a second spanner is needed, and sometimes locking pins are used. High quality routers also have a locking mechanism which is tightened to lock the motor spindle while changing the tool. In this case, apart from the spanner for the chuck nut, no other tool is needed.

To make fitting of the new cutter easy, lower the machine to the stop in the frame. Important: the shank must be inserted at least 20 mm into the collet, to achieve a secure hold. Under no circumstances must this minimum value be reduced, for instance, to achieve a deeper cut.

After the cutter has been inserted, lock the motor spindle again and tighten the chuck nut. But do not tighten the nut if there is no cutter in the collet chuck — this would damage the tool receptacle. If you want to insert a cutter with a different shank diameter, turn the clamping nut to the left until the complete collet chuck can be loosened and exchanged.

Adjusting the routing depth

Before each new router operation, the required cutting depth must be exactly set. Routers have different facilities to preselect or adjust the cutting depth. Some can be modified in steps according to a programme.

The cutting result is always better if a minimum of material is removed in one operation. There will be also less strain on the bit. Depending on application, always make several cuts, with the last operation removing the least material.

Adjustment of the required depth always starts by lowering the machine until the cutter touches the workpiece

For setting the cutting depth, release the framework locking mechanism and lower the motor part until the cutter touches the workpiece. If the router has a stop block, choose the lowest setting. Now lower the actual stop block until it rests on the workpiece. Depending on the machine, there are scales or setting devices, which allow the stop block to be raised by exactly the amount which corresponds to the required cutting depth.

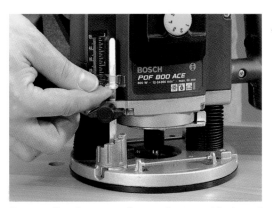

For rough adjustment lower the stop block and then raise it again according to the intended cutting depth and lock into position

Now, when plunging the cutter into the workpiece, the router motor can be lowered until the stop block rests again and the chosen depth has been reached. Very often, absolute cutting precision is essential. Therefore, good routers have a precision adjustment, which, after a first test cut, allows the setting to be corrected to 0.1 mm accuracy.

If the step guide is used, turn it back by one or more settings according to the base setting as described. Then the stop block reaches only the higher step during the first operation and correspondingly little material is taken off. Step by step the cutting depth is increased, until the final depth is reached. The router shown above has the facility for operation in eight steps.

After the rough setting, carry out a test cut. With routers with precision adjustment, it can be readjusted to within 0.1 mm

At the front edge of a workpiece, always move the router from left to right — against the cutter turning circle

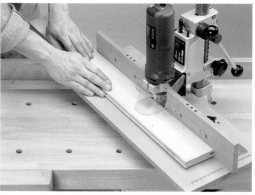

If a board's back edge is cut in a router stand, move it from left to right. This is reversed when cutting the front

With cutting, movement must be steady and swift. Ugly burn marks appear if the cutter turns too long in one place

Golden rules for routing

If worked on expertly — this includes using high quality tools — the wood surface shows a perfect cutting finish. Tools must be sharp and the bits undamaged. After a job is done, the expert stores the cleaned cutters in a stand and takes care that the cutting edges do not get into contact with other metal parts.

Your router should have the facility to pre-select the revolutions and guarantee electronically controlled motor torque under load. With this specification, the ideal speed for each operation is maintained. A further luxury feature, this controller allows a smooth start — so avoiding notching which could occur with a jerky start.

Take care with the cutting depth! Adjust your router so that the revolutions are maintained; for a good cutting finish, swift forward movement is also important. Be happy with relatively little material removal per operation. Indeed, take a number of cuts. Burn marks on the wood indicate where the router was moved along too slowly.

A further golden rule of routing is: always move the machine against the rotation direction of the router (contra-rotation). This means move your router along the workpiece front from left to right, so the material is removed smoothly. The machine can be snatched out of your hand, if you move the workpiece in the same direction as the rotation of the cutter. Also the cutting finish will be poor because the cutter edges hit the material. If the router is used in a router stand, the direction to push depends on whether the workpiece front or back edge is brought to the cutter. If the back edge is worked on, move the part from left to right; when cutting the front edge, from right to left.

Safety

To protect against injuries, always switch off and isolate the router when changing cutters or working on the motor spindle. Insert cutter shank at least 20 mm into the collet and tighten well!

Clamp workpieces and templates well, to avoid the router tilting during forward move.

Ensure that the electric cable to the router is well out of the way when cutting.

First position the router on or against the workpiece, then start the motor. Release the router framework locking mechanism and plunge the motor until the stop block is reached. Then secure again and move the router along steadily and swiftly. At the end of each operation, the motor part must be moved up before the router is removed from the workpiece. Then switch off.

Throughout all routing operations, safety glasses and clothing with close-fitting sleeves should be worn. Wide sleeves can get caught while the router is moved forward and if the machine tilts, there is a risk that the cutter could cause injury.

Dust dangerous for health can develop when cutting chipboard and MDF, but also when working with oak or beech. Therefore, if possible, cut only with a dust extractor connected and in operation.

Safety rule number 1, which must be observed under all circumstances: first disconnect electric cable, then change the cutter

The workpiece must be firmly secured with clamps or cramps to the carpenter's bench, before the router is positioned

Dust produced from wood or wood materials can endanger health. Therefore, modern routers are equipped with a dust extractor connection

Furniture for children

Robust furniture for children is often particularly expensive. Here, we propose a design where each part only costs a few pounds. The trick we use: cheap planed timber is glued and nailed together to form solid laminated boards and is structurally joined at the same time.

A DIY beginner will probably not venture to tackle a difficult joint. As a start we have therefore developed a design, based on a simple principle, to build nicely proportioned, and at the same time extremely strong, furniture for children. The timber, which we select as material, is particularly cheap! For example, the stool cost approximately £8. The strips are glued together in layers. In this way, a bridle corner joint can be made without special skills.

First, cut the strips for one unit — dimensions and number according to the parts list. However, wherever the strips overlap — for example at the corners or at the backrest — you must select the correct components to assemble the interlocking joints. (a) the furniture overall dimension or (b) for the leg: 'outer dimension minus strip width' or (c) for the top: 'outer dimension minus double strip width'. The drawings on page 25 clearly show the construction principle.

For assembly, put the first layer in right angles onto the workbench. The parts must butt accurately. Then apply glue with a brush. At intervals of 50 mm, hammer in 35 mm long pins into the second layer so that the points protrude a little from the underside. When putting on the next strip, edge flush, it will not slip and the pins can easily be hammered in. The same steps are repeated until the last layer. Here, the nail heads must be countersunk and filled.

When the piece of furniture has been assembled, carefully sand the surfaces. Slightly round the outer edges using the router and ovolo cutter. A guide roller guarantees an even cutting finish. Finally, rub furniture wax suitable for children over the surface.

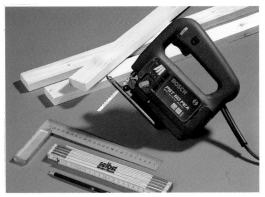

Measure the planed timber and mark out with a carpenter's set square. Then cut cleanly with a jigsaw

The construction joint is achieved by applying glue to each layer and nailing. The last nails are countersunk

Turn strips with faulty edges so that they point to the furniture underside. Smooth the surface with an orbital sander

Children's furniture should not have sharp edges. With the use of the router, carefully round the outer edges. An ovolo cutter with guide roller ensures an even cutting finish

Before surface treatment, once again carefully sand the wood. Even the rounded edges are smoothed without difficulty with an eccentric disc sander

After hand-sanding with 240 grit paper, apply the wax. If necessary, the wood can be sanded and waxed again later

Parts list

	Number	Name	Dimensions, mm	Material
Table	8	Leg components	530 long	Planed
	4	Leg components	485 long	timber
	22	Tabletop components	800 long	45 × 20 mm
	4	Tabletop components	710 long	
Bench	8	Leg components	305 long	Planed
	4	Leg components	260 long	timber
	13	Seat components	660 long	45 × 20 mm
	4	Seat components	570 long	
Stool	8	Leg components	305 long	Planed
	4	Leg components	260 long	timber
	13	Seat components	380 long	45 × 20 mm
	4	Seat components	290 long	
Chair	6	Leg components	305 long	Planed
	2	Leg components	260 long	timber
	2	Leg components	550 long	
	8	Seat components	380 long	45 × 20 mm
	5	Seat components	.335 long	
	4	Seat components	290 long	
	5	Back rest components	290 long	
	6	Back rests	245 long	

Panel pins 35 mm, wood filler, glue

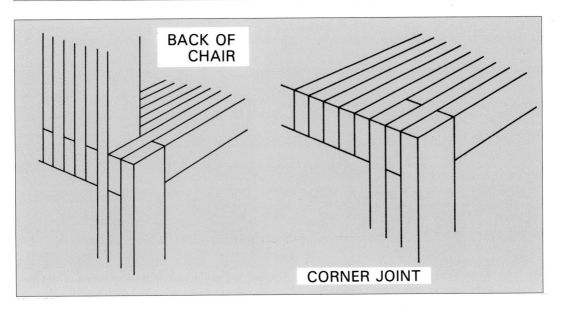

BACK OF CHAIR

CORNER JOINT

The chair: the legs and also the back rest are firmly joined with the seat by gluing strips of different lengths

The stool is the simplest part in our furniture set. This also gets its strength by alternate gluing of strips

The table: because of the relatively large area, the tabletop can easily be uneven after gluing. Therefore, if necessary, plane flat the surface before sanding

The bench: except for the seat length, construction of the bench is exactly the same as for the stool. Because of its dimensions, as well as for nursery use, it can also be used as a plant stand

Furniture for sitting and playing on, constructed in no time for little money. All you need is a few bundles of planed timber, available at every builders' merchant

Cot

Children's furniture should not only be robust and
practical – its design must please the little
users and stimulate their imagination. The ideal
material is, of course, treated manufactured board.
Our cot takes all this into account.

How do you convince children that it is time to go to bed? With a lot of persuasion, would you agree? Perhaps, a nice cot would also do the trick: our novel design is made from solid beech blockboard which because it is so strong, can serve as sleeping accommodation for generations. With base dimensions of 140 × 70 cm, the cot offers ample space. Very young babies may appear a little lost and they ought to lie a little higher for easier lifting out and putting back to bed. To use the cot during your baby's first year, simply screw a backing board to the inside of the front sun motif, and fix to this a horizontal rail to support a slatted mattress frame. Your baby will then lie at a higher level.

For children who can crawl, the bed offers an opening at the foot, where they can slip through and start exploring. The flap is secured from outside by just two dowels with knobs, which are pushed through the corner board into corresponding holes in the blockboard. When lowered, the flap becomes a comfortable 'crawling ramp'.

Here are the construction details. Two frame assemblies form the basis for the cot. They are made from 26 mm beech blockboard. The frame boards are connected by means of slots and flat dowels. To gain more strength, we have always set two flat dowels on top of each other, so the joint is especially firm and the large glue area guarantees highest strength. Slots for the dowels can be made precisely with the stationary mounted router. Use the slotting cutter, lower the router to the required height and bring the workpiece to it. Once set, you can repeatedly make, all at the same height, as many slots as are required. Always cut the slots sideways a little larger than absolutely required to give some clearance for assembling. When cutting into the end, the workpiece is flat on the router

The semicircular section for the sun is marked out with dividers then cut out with a jigsaw

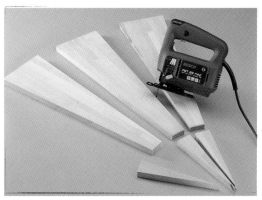

Cut out the rays, put the sun insert on top and mark the radius, cut out with the jigsaw

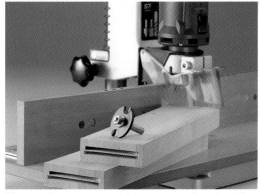

The stationary mounted router, equipped with a slotting cutter cuts slots for the flat dowels into the frame boards

One front frame corner before applying glue. The construction is joined together without problem by using flat dowels

After sanding the beech wood, rub in primer oil. The next day apply the wax by cloth

table. For cutting into the side, it must stand vertically on its end. As it can easily tilt sideways, it is better to clamp on an additional piece at the side to increase the support area. Cut 6 mm grooves into the blockboard of the back frame where the plywood panels (parts 12 and 13) are inserted. At the front, the sun and rays must be fitted before the individual parts are glued together.

The semicircular sun is easily cut with a jigsaw. Use the table circular saw or a portable one with guide to make the 'rays', and fit these into the outer frame. Assemble without glue. Cut slots for the flat dowels which are used here for jointing. When all the parts have been prepared, the whole assembly is glued together. If sufficiently long cramps are not available, lay the frame onto a supporting construction made of slats and wedge tightly after the glue has been applied. Be careful to maintain all right angles.

The ray motif is continued with a semicircular piece at the top front edge. This is also fixed with flat dowels. The bed's head and end cross rails are also easily joined with flat dowels. But if you want to easily dismantle the bed, use removable screws instead. For this, fit threaded dowels into the cross rails and then drill matching through holes into the corner leg boards to fit round headed securing metal thread screws. The flap at the foot is supported on two dowels, which locate in matching holes in the corner boards. Two further dowels with wooden knobs are used to fasten the board in its closed position.

The slatted mattress frame can be made either from softwood strips or bought ready-made. Finally, treat the beech blockboard with oil or wax suitable for children.

Parts list

No.	Quantity	Name	Dimension, mm	Material
1	4	Corner leg boards	820 long	Beech blockboard
2	3	Side rails	1260 × 80	26 mm
3	2	Side rails	1260 × 100	
4	1	Cross rails	700 × 100	
5	3	Cross rails	700 × 80	
6	1	Cross rail	700 × 60	
7	1	Flap	696 × 395	
8	1	Semicircle	200 diameter	
9	1	Sun insert	400 diameter	Beech blockboard
10	2	Support rails	1400 × 19	19 mm
11	2	Support rails	662 × 19	
12	1	Side panel	1280 × 300	Beech plywood
13	1	End panel	720 × 300	6 mm
14	2	Knobs	20 thick	Ø 35 mm

4 dowels Ø 10 × 90 mm (flap support and fixing) 2 wooden knobs, flat dowels.
All sun ray inserts, made of 19 mm beech blockboard, are individually positioned and cut to size.
For safety reasons, the maximum gap between the rays should not exceed 110 mm.

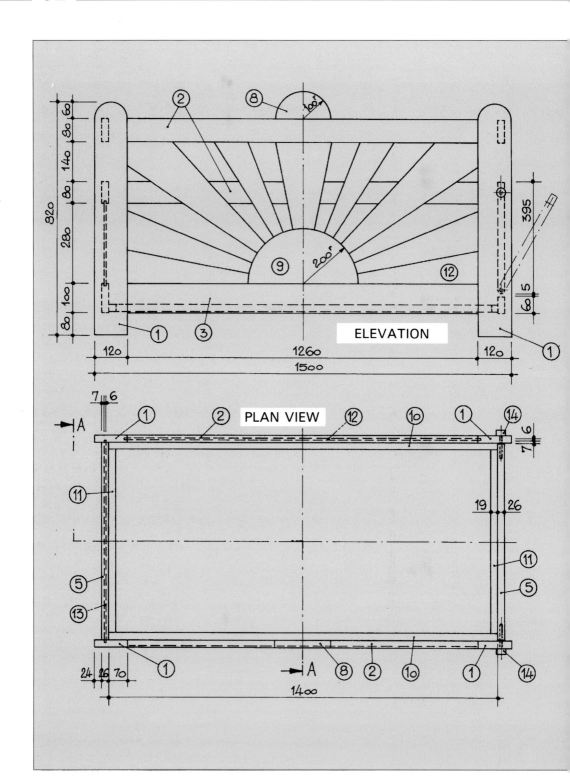

ELEVATION

PLAN VIEW

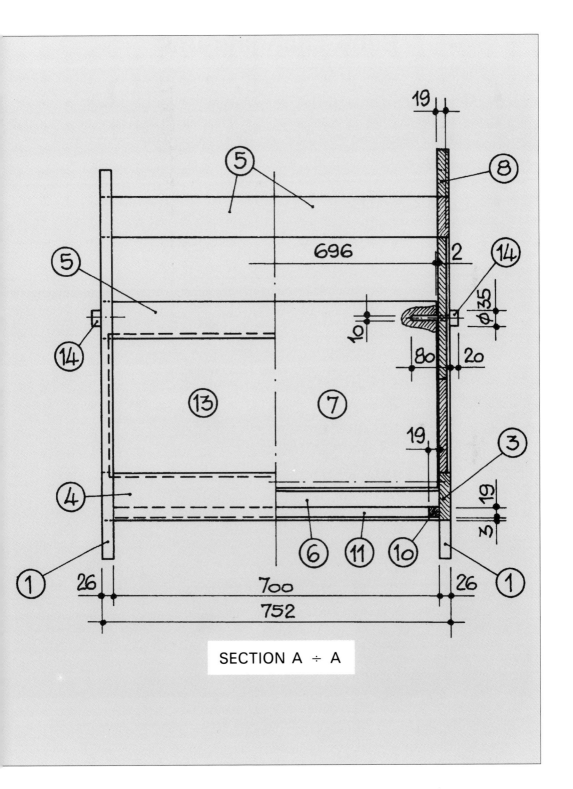

SECTION A ÷ A

Baby changing unit

Besides the cot, the nursery needs a changing unit
for daily care of newly borns. Here is a changing
unit, matching the sun-ray bed, also made from
beech blockboard and with the sun motif.

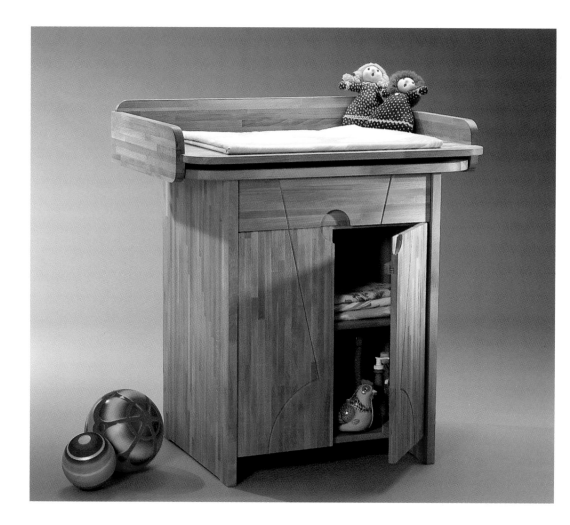

Practical children's furniture should be constructed for possibly many years of use. A changing unit, which is only used until the child has grown out of nappies, is too expensive for short term investment. We propose constructing the actual changing unit as a top, which slides onto the chest and can easily be removed, if necessary. Without the top this is a nice chest of drawers, which will also fit into a teenager's room or could be integrated into any other part of the living area.

Cut the individual parts according to the dimensions given in the parts list on page 41. If you do not have a table or portable circular saw, you can fall back upon the cutting service offered by many do-it-yourself supermarkets or timber merchants. Work is continued in your own workshop, where, besides other power tools, the router is of great importance.

We have used dovetailed housing joints for the carcass. With this wood joining technique, a bevelled edge is cut into both sides of a board's front end, so the board section looks like a dovetail. The mating board is given a dovetail section groove, using the same angles. The dovetailed edge can then slide into this groove and both parts are firmly joined to each other, distortion-free. There is no need to glue. Due to the form of the dovetailed housing joint, the two workpieces are absolutely firm without glue. If necessary, it can even be dismantled, for example, to save space during transport.

We start the work on both side walls (1). First, 6 mm rebates are cut into the back edges, these take the plywood back panel. For this, guide the router with a straight fence or use a rebate cutter with guide roller. The guide roller below the bit follows the board edge precisely and guarantees

A rebate is cut into the rear edges of the side panels for the insertion of the plywood back panel. Rebates for the bottom shelf are cut in the same way

The dovetailed housing joint is made with bevel and dovetail cutters. Here dovetailing of a side wall, using a temporary fence

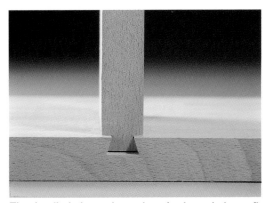

The detailed photo shows how both workpieces fit together in an extremely strong dovetailed housing joint

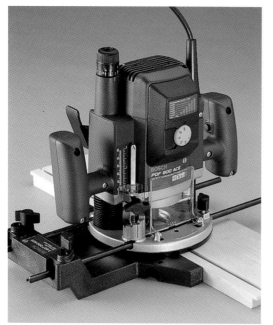

Grooves for inserting the plywood bottom are cut into the drawer sides, which also have rebated tongues to fit grooves in the drawer front and back panels

The finger recess for drawer front and both doors is made with a circular cut in one operation

an even cutting finish. The next operation is to mark the positions where the boards (5) and (6) are fixed to the side walls using rebated housing joints. Fit a dovetail cutter to the router and attach a fence onto the workpiece parallel to the planned groove. The first cut removes only as much material as the width of the cutter. To achieve the groove width for receiving the cross board tongue a second cut will probably be necessary. The joints should remain invisible at the front of the chest, so set both groove rebate and the mating tongue about one centimetre away from the side wall front edge. Allow 0.5 mm clearance between tongue and groove, so that both parts can easily be pushed into each other.

The underside of the top also has two rebated grooves, to which the upper edges of the side walls will be fitted. After all the grooves have been made, the tongues are cut in the matching facing edges. To do this, guide the router vertically along the straight fence. It is best to clamp the workpiece. As with all difficult cutting jobs, try the router adjustment first on some trial wood before working on the actual piece.

Before the carcass is put together, bore holes into the side walls: for the loose shelf support and also for the concealed hinges for hanging the doors.

When the carcass is complete, the back panel is screwed in and construction of the drawer and doors commences. To make the continuous decoration for the drawer front and doors, fix the three parts together to the workbench and first cut the straight lines using an 8 mm cove cutter. Guide the router along a temporary fence. For the curved lines use the circular guide and set a 20 cm radius. The router should plunge

Without the changing unit and decorative piece at the back of the top, the chest makes an elegant piece of furniture anywhere in the living area

A single manipulation changes it into a baby changing unit: the outer edges of the chest top slide into the two grooves in the fixture

about 5 mm deep into the wood.

The finger recess for drawer and doors is cut with the router in one operation. With the aid of a groove cutter a circular template and a template guide cut a circular recess, 90 mm diameter and 10 mm deep, around the point where the three parts meet. Next, the cove cutter is put into use again. It is positioned on the recess bottom. Then fix the cutting depth and 'undercut' the edge of the circular section until the cutter shank touches the upper remaining recess edge.

The drawer is made to classic rules. The side pieces have rebates, which are glued into corresponding housing grooves in the drawer front and back. The plywood bottom fits into a 6 mm groove, which is 8 mm from the lower edge so the bottom can be inserted into the assembled drawer through the shallower back.

Both doors are fitted with concealed hinges, before we finally start with the changing unit fixture. Again, side pieces and top are joined using the dovetail housing joint, whilst the back board is fixed with dowels. A 27 mm parallel groove on the inner side of the side piece is needed to slide the fixture onto the chest top. Although it juts far out at the front, the unit is completely safely joined to the base. If required, a decorative top may be added to the chest top – this continues the ornamental cutting line of the front.

Treat the surface as for the cot with oil followed by wax.

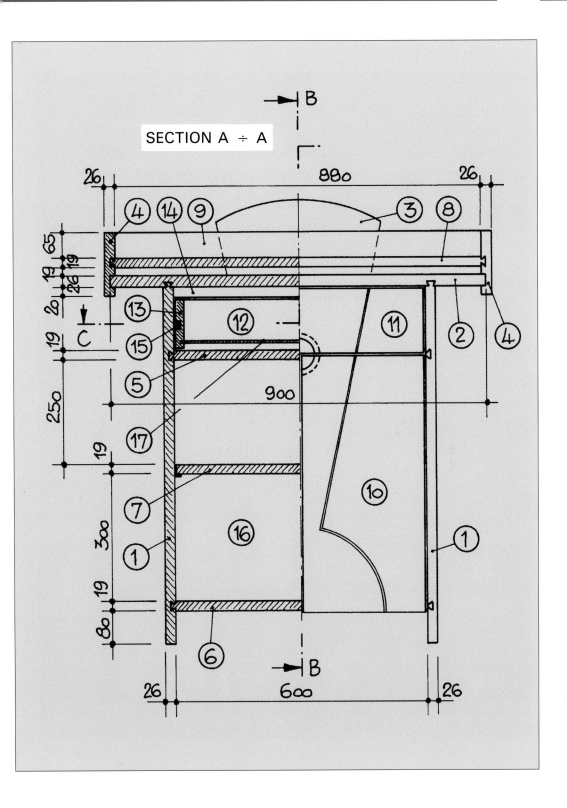

SECTION A ÷ A

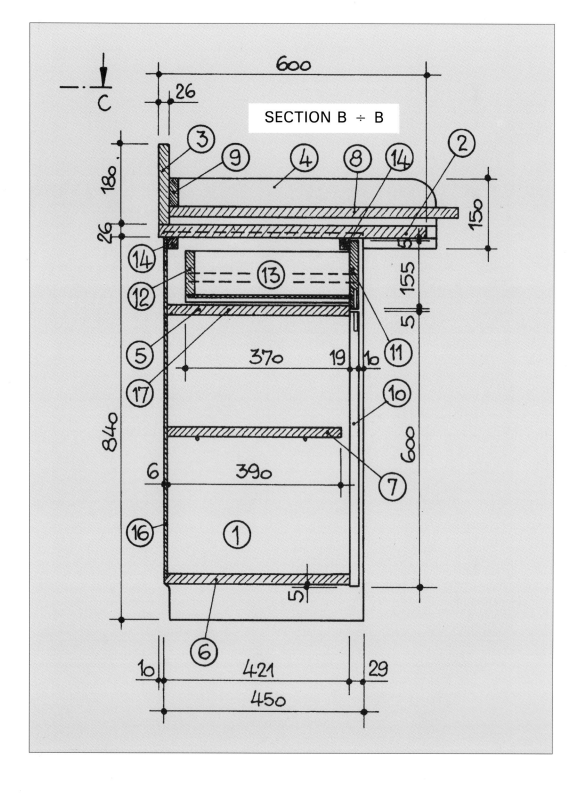

SECTION B ÷ B

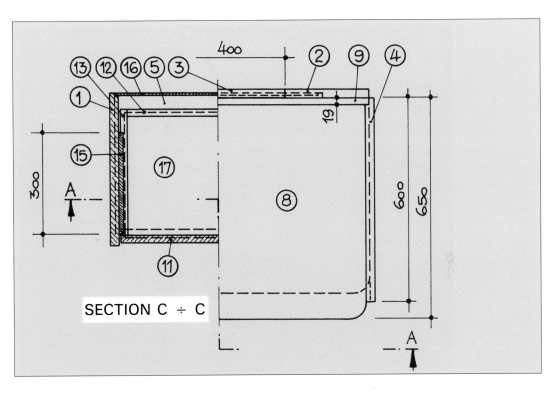

SECTION C ÷ C

Parts list

No.	Quantity	Name	Dimensions, mm	Material
1	2	Side walls	850 × 450	Beech blockboard
2	1	Main top	900 × 600	26 mm thick
3	1	Decorative top	400 × 180	
4	2	Side rails	600 × 150	
5	1	Under drawer board	620 × 415	Beech blockboard
6	1	Bottom board	620 × 421	19 mm thick
7	1	Loose shelf	598 × 390	
8	1	Changing unit base	900 × 600	
9	1	Changing unit back	900 × 65	
10	2	Doors	600 × 296	
11	1	Drawer front	596 × 155	
12	1	Drawer back	558 × 110	
13	2	Drawer sides	370 × 124	
14	2	Main top supports	600 × 19	
15	2	Runners	300 long	Beech, 20 × 15 mm
16	1	Back panel	830 × 620	6 mm plywood
17	1	Drawer bottom	578 × 375	

2 pairs of concealed hinges for inset doors; 4 shelf supports; chipboard screws; glue

Tree coat stand

Keeping things tidy need not be tiresome. Proof of this is our smart coat stand for children. Using cheap plywood or blockboard, this gem for children is quickly made and, as our instructions show, no special skills are required.

The daily battle for a slightly more tidy children's room is known to all parents. Little ones, coming home from play or school, are prone to simply throw to the floor things like cap and anorak. Many hall stand hooks are at heights inaccessible for children. What's missing is a coat stand inside the children's room. Not just coat hooks simply screwed to the wall — something attractive is needed to educate a child to be tidy.

Our 'tree coat stand' is ideal. It is constructed in no time and your offspring will be filled with enthusiasm. You will need two 19 mm plywood/blockboard sheets, either spruce or pine. The trunk of the 'tree coat stand' is cut from a sheet 40 × 120 cm. For the top, a nominal size of 60 × 90 cm is required.

With the help of the grid on page 44, the contours of trunk and treetop can easily be transferred onto the board. One square on the drawing corresponds to 10 × 10 cm actual size. Therefore, mark the plywood area with 10 cm squares, using a fine pencil. Then transfer, square by square, the contours of the coat stand as shown on the drawing.

It is best to cut the top first, then put this onto the sheet for the trunk and mark out the contours where both parts overlap. Very good results are achieved if the plywood is cut with a jigsaw equipped with a special blade for curves.

After cutting, the edges must be tackled. In order to achieve an even rounding, the router equipped with an ovolo is used. A guide roller mounted on the router makes sure that an equal distance to the edge is maintained. Then, as shown on the drawing, drill seven 14 mm holes into the tree top for taking the hooks.

After transferring the trunk and treetop outlines onto the plywood, the contours are sawn with a jigsaw using a blade for curves

The edges of the plywood parts can be evenly rounded with help of a router and ovolo with guide roller

The hooks, made from suitable round wood sections, are set into the seven 14 mm bore holes in the treetop

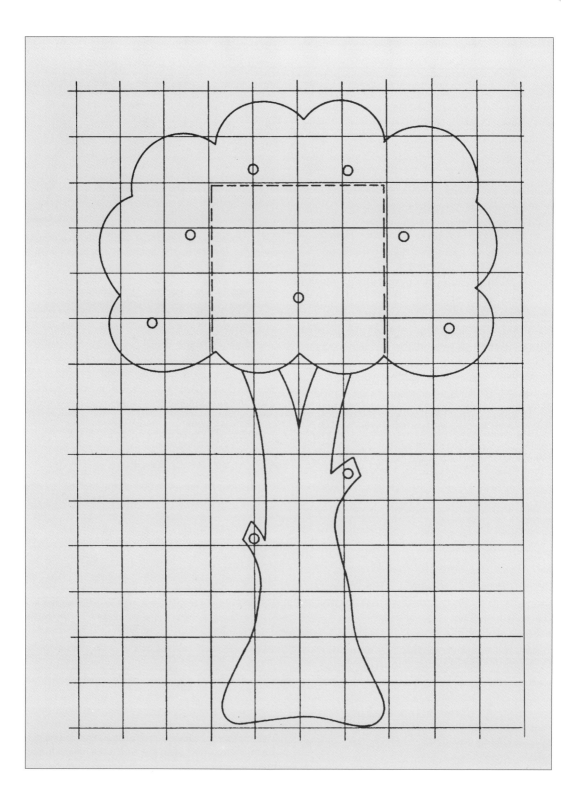

The hooks themselves consist of round wood sections, the notches are cut on a wood turning lathe, to the dimensions as shown on the detailed drawing below. Alternatively, carve the notches if you do not have a lathe.

When the parts have been prepared, commence staining or painting. Use only non-toxic paints. Then, glue the hooks into the holes and from the back, screw the top to the trunk. If the tree coat stand rests firmly on the floor, one wood screw with 8 mm dowel in the top centre is sufficient for fastening to the wall.

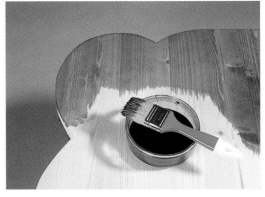

By using coloured stain, the wood grain remains visible. Apply the stain with a wide brush, wet on wet

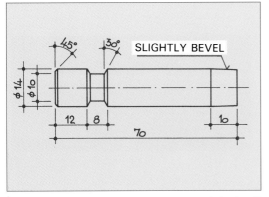

The detail drawing shows the section of the hook. Either use a lathe or notch with a wood carving knife

Finally, from the back, connect trunk and top with 35 mm long self-cutting wood screws

Parts list

No.	Quantity	Name	Dimensions, mm	Material
1	1	Trunk	1200 × 400	Pine plywood/blockboard
2	1	Treetop	900 × 600	19 mm thick
3	9	Hooks	70 long	14 mm diameter dowelling

Coloured wood stain; chipboard screws; glue

Chest of drawers

You can never have enough drawers. This elegant chest provides as many as eight in designer style. Although the construction has some craftsmanship refinements, it is not difficult to make. The router is fully involved using all its technical facilities.

Since blockboard is available in different sheet thicknesses and format, it is no longer a problem to build solid wood furniture using classic cabinet-making techniques. Besides spruce and pine, precious wood has also been available for a long time in blockboard which is easy to handle. For our captivatingly designed slimline chest of drawers we have chosen American maple. The coloured base and top and the handles are made from MDF (medium-density fibreboard). This manufactured board can be routed in a similar manner to natural timber.

The exploded diagrams on page 50 explains the construction. Start with cutting the blockboard parts to size — dimensions to be found in the parts list. The carcass parts and drawer sides are easily cut with a circular saw. More arduous, but not less precise, cutting is achieved with a portable circular saw which is guided along a fixed fence (it can be fixed with cramps) or a special aluminium rail.

The side panels receive 8 grooves each to accept the side runners. The router is guided by a clamped on fence

After the individual parts have been prepared continue to work on the side panels. Here, the router comes into action three times. The first operation cuts rebates into the back edges for accepting the back panel. The next step cuts dowel holes, which are needed for fixing the bottom panels and drawer rails. Here, the router proves how precisely it can work. Because of the base-plate, exact vertical plunging is guaranteed.

When working close to workpiece edges, a suitable piece of waste-wood must be used at the side to support the router baseplate and ensure that it does not tilt over the edge. When making dowel holes, set the stop block so that the dowels have 2 mm air clearance at the bottom of the hole. This leaves space for surplus glue and it ensures that the parts to be joined are assembled without problem.

The side runners must not be fixed with glue. They are fixed with countersunk wood screws to allow the wood to work

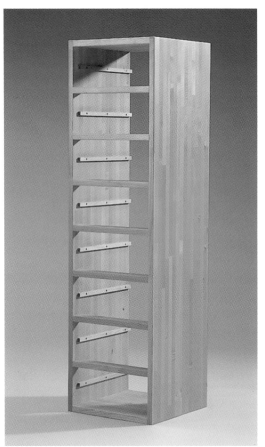

The carcass is assembled from side panels, bottom panels and drawer rails. All joints are dowelled and glued flush

The four drawer sides are joined with dowels and glue. Cramp the parts together

The third operation on the side panels is to cut grooves for accepting the side runners, on which the drawers will slide later on. Cut 12 mm wide grooves spaced to give exact clearance for the drawers in their housing. Stop the grooves 30 mm from the front end and chisel a right angle afterwards. The drawer side grooves are set back by the same 30 mm so that the closed drawer is flush with the carcass.

Do not glue the side runners into the grooves. The grain of side panel and runner runs exactly against each other, so the blockboard could develop tension cracks while the panels are still drying out. This is likely to be a problem with kiln dried blockboard. Therefore fix the runners with chipboard screws. Pre-drill the holes and countersink so that the screw heads will not project. For this work, a battery-operated drill would be very useful.

After the side panels are complete, we start with the two bottom panels. These also get a rebate at the back end. As the dowel holes are drilled into the edges, it would be preferable to add a dowel template, to plunge exactly at a right angle into the wood. Now, only the seven drawer rails are missing to complete the carcass. They are also inserted with dowels and for this, drill two holes into each of the face edges.

Apply glue to side panels, bottom panels and drawer rails and join by means of the dowels. Using large cramps, press the parts together until the glue has set. Take care, that bottom and side panels are rectangular. The back panel is only put in after the drawers have been completed and fitted. The already cut-to-size drawer sides are equipped with dowel holes for later assembly, but before this, they get a groove running parallel to the lower edge, into which the plywood drawer bottoms can be inserted. Cut the grooves by using a router and a straight fence. To make this work easier, you could cut the grooves first into the boards and then cut out the drawer sides/back/front.

If you want to save material costs, you may use high quality hardwood for the drawer fronts only. For sides and back, pine can also be used as these parts are not visible. When gluing the drawers take care that the parts are in a right angle. Either check with a large try-square or, even better, measure the diagonals of the drawers. They must show exactly the same measurement.

In the next operation, the prepared drawers receive the grooves in which the side runners slide. For this, use the router and straight fence. As already mentioned, the grooves must not continue to the end as they also form the stop for the drawers.

The router is used once again to cut mortises for the handles. A temporary fence, fitted at an angle of 45 degree to the edge, takes care of exact guidance. The handles are cut as semicircles. Use an ovolo with guide pin for rounding so that the handles fit exactly into the slots. Of course, you can form the handles to your own ideas or use ready-made wooden or metal items.

When carcass and drawers are complete, most of the work is done. Only the MDF base and top are missing. The 22 mm thick square and oblong are first cut to size and then base and top edges are slightly rounded using a large ovolo cutter. Fasten the parts with screws from the inside of the carcass. But before this, the chest must be painted and varnished. As the face edges of MDF are strongly absorbent,

When gluing the drawers make sure that all sides are rectangular. It is best to measure and compare the diagonals

The runner grooves, stopped at the front, are cut into the drawer sides. Guide the machine with a straight fence

Base and top edges are also rounded with the ovolo. Do this in two operations

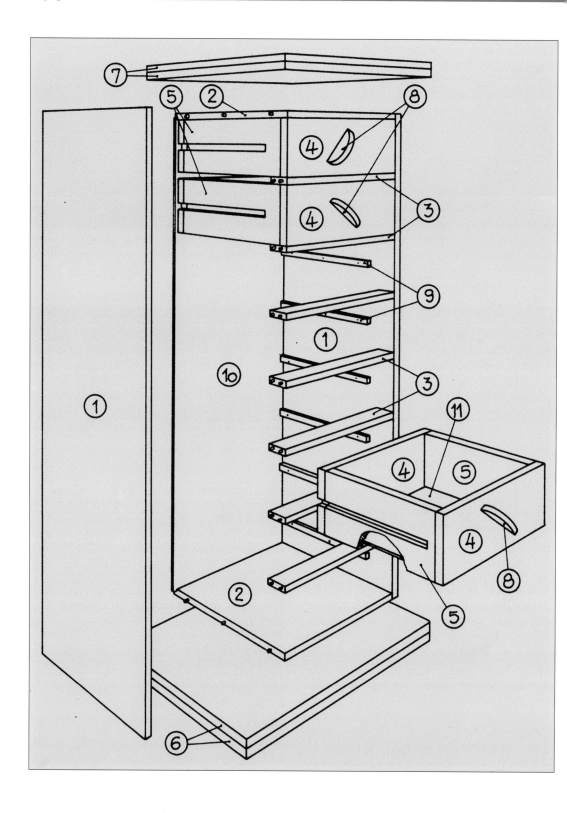

seal the material first with a two-pack lacquer. Then sand again and paint the surface with a colour of your choice.

The blockboard surfaces of carcass and drawers can be treated with a clear varnish, wax or oil. The optimum surface build up is as follows: first rub in an undercoat oil until saturated. The next day when the oil has been fully absorbed, rub again with a soft cloth before wax is applied with a linen cloth.

A well known tip to make drawers smooth running: grease all side runners with candle wax, they will slide almost by themselves.

The work was worthwhile. The chest of drawers represents a top modern design and is also practical

Material list

No.	Quantity	Name	Dimensions, mm	Material
1	2	Side panels	1190 × 340	19 mm
2	2	Bottom panels	303 × 340	American
3	7	Drawer rails	303 × 45	maple
4	16	Drawer fronts/backs	300 × 125	
5	16	Drawer sides	296 × 125	
6	2	Base	550 × 450	22 mm MDF
7	2	Top	450 × 450	
8	8	Handles	115 long	MDF 40 × 19 mm
9	16	Side runners	305 long	Maple 15 × 12 mm
10	1	Back panel	1172 × 322	5 mm Gaboon
11	8	Drawer bottoms	292 × 276	plywood
Chipboard screws; dowels Ø 8 × 40 mm; glue				

Double bed and bedside table

Clear lines, exclusive design. This attractive double bed is more than just a practical piece of furniture. Material: beech blockboard and coloured painted MDF. There are also two tastefully designed matching bedside tables.

Double bed

Our do-it-yourself double bed equally con-vinces by its sleeping comfort and its elegant appearance. Reason enough to venture to construct it. Following our instructions, the cabinet-making task is achieved without major problems. We also present the matching bedside table which goes with it. With these, your bedroom furnishing is almost complete.

The drawing on page 56 shows clearly the bed's design principle. It consists of head and foot components and two side rails. An out-of-sight centre support is added for the mattress slats. This support is fastened with two dowels (without glue) at the head.

Keyhole plates are let into the four legs to connect the side rails with head and foot boards. This precision work will turn out especially well if a router is used. A 20 mm rebate cutter with the router guided by a temporary fence provide the necessary recess. Square off the corners with a chisel to ensure the oblong mountings fit. Insert two round head screws each into the rail faces at either end. These are fitted into the keyhole plate openings. In this way, the bed is easily assembled and disassembled when necessary.

First prepare the timber. From the parts list it can be seen which parts are required and their dimensions. If you do not have a table circular saw, use a portable circular saw with fence. First construct the legs (1) from two 19 mm MDF boards glued together. The initially rectangular shape is cut down later so that the legs are standing on the floor sloping inwards at an angle of 85 degrees. The upper slope is cut to an angle of 45 degrees. Slightly chamfer all visible outer edges with the router. Now

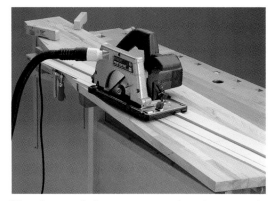

The slopes of the upper cross boards are made with a portable circular saw. Use a rail or fence as guide

Using a router, chamfer the visible edges before gluing. As shown in the photo, accurate guidance is achieved with the attachment to the cutter front

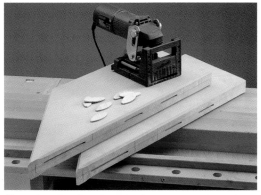

Slots for the flat dowel joints are made without problem with a cutter attached to the angle grinder

This device will help to glue head and foot boards: fix two blocks of wood to a board (about 2.5 m) and cramp the whole using wedges

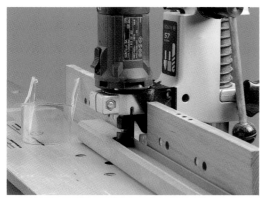

The MDF capping strips receive a 10 mm deep and 27 mm wide groove. For this, mount the router firmly into the stand

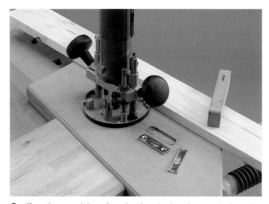

Scribe the position for the keyhole plates and make recesses with a 20 mm rebate cutter. Open up the corners with a chisel

cut parts (7) and (8) from 26 mm blockboard. Boards (6) and (8) form the gable shape for head and foot of the bed. They slope down from the middle to 250 mm at the outer edges.

The four end faces of the cross boards (5) and (7) must also be sloped at 85 degrees to match the legs. To exactly mark out the slopes lay the parts, which are slightly oversized, onto the legs lying flat on the floor and lined up against a strip. Parts (5) and (6) must be laid at 230 and 700 mm respectively from the leg lower edge. For parts (7) and (8) these dimensions are 50 and 350 mm.

When the cross boards have been marked out and cut to size, they are joined to the legs. Here, we decided to use loose flat dowels. This joint provides a very large glue line which guarantees maximum strength. With the right tool, very exact cutting of the slots is achieved. For example, an angle grinder with cutter attachment could be used.

After the head and foot boards are joined, capping strips (13) and (14) and also the decorative knobs (3) must still be made. The capping strips are machined to a U-profile, so they can be fitted onto the upper cross boards. Guide the strips along the stationary mounted router and with a rebate cutter make a 10 mm deep and 27 mm wide groove.

The decorative knobs are three 19 mm MDF discs of 60 mm diameter glued together. Before gluing together, cut a sector out of the middle disc, which fits exactly onto the points of parts (6) and (8). After gluing, increase the width of the resulting groove with a chisel to 27 mm, the knobs can then be fitted onto the cross boards in the same way as the capping strips. Now, saw the capping strips exactly to fit and glue together with the decorative knobs. Now, head and foot parts are complete. Finally, as already described, fit the keyhole plates into the legs.

For the next step, the side rails (4) are cut to size. Screw round head screws in to fit the keyhole plates in the legs. Two strips (9), fixed with screws, serve as support for the mattress slats or spring frame. The slats or frame have a support in the middle of the bed. A board (12), cut from a 19 mm softwood plank, is the actual support, which rests on 5 support legs. Two dowels join the head support leg (10) to the head piece.

After all parts have been completed, commence the surface treatment. Apply coloured paint to all MDF parts and clear varnish to the blockboard parts.

Round head screws in the side rails are hung into the leg keyhole plates. Support rails carry the spring frame or slats

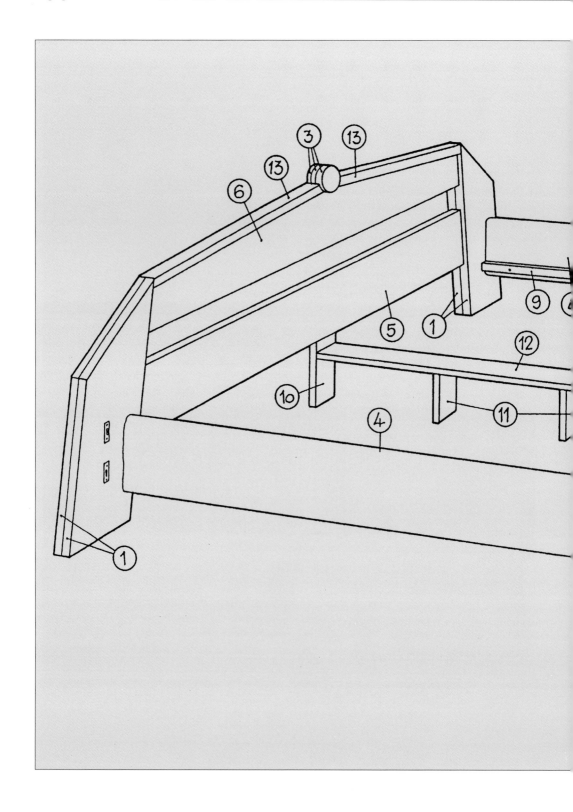

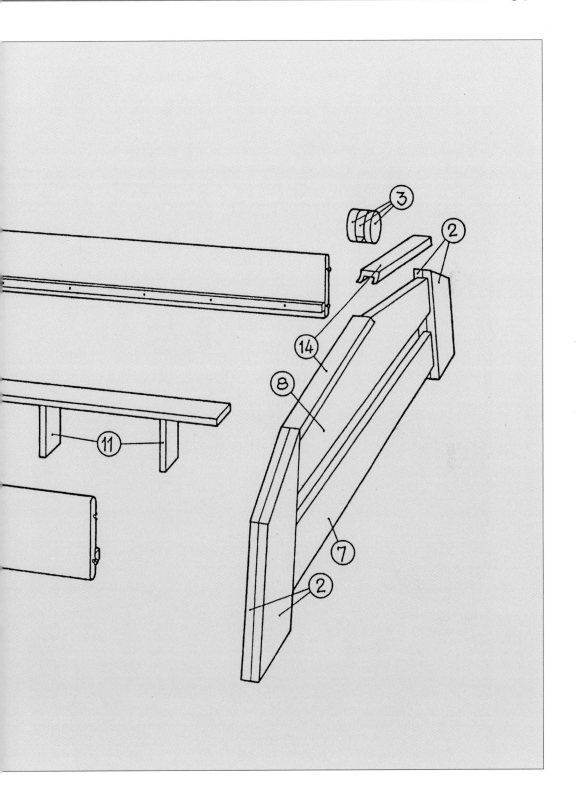

Parts list

No.	Quantity	Name	Dimensions, mm	Material
1	4	Legs	843 × 246	19 mm MDF
2	4	Legs	693 × 246	
3	6	Knob components	Ø 60	
4	2	Side rails	2000 × 250	26 mm Beech
5	1	Head board component	1778 × 290	blockboard
6	1	Head board component	1646 × 288	
7	1	Foot board component	1816 × 250	
8	1	Foot board component	1708 × 290	
9	2	Slat/spring frame side support	2000 × 40	
10	1	Head board centre support	230 × 100	
11	4	Slat centre support legs	176 × 100	
12	1	Slat centre support	1995 × 100	19 mm soft wood plank
13	2	Capping strips	810 long*	MDF
14	2	Capping strips	830 long*	40 × 30 mm

8 keyhole plates 70 × 20 mm; chipboard screws; flat dowels; dowels; glue (* = nominal dimension)

Bedside table

Even the most beautiful bed is incomplete without a matching bedside table. After all, clock, lamp and books must be put down somewhere. And, if at the weekend the alarm clock remains silent, breakfast in bed is a possibility. Space for the breakfast tray is a necessity.

The bedside tables presented offer a very special comfort: their tops are supported by a special rotary fitting. So, for example at Sunday breakfast, the cup can easily be brought to a comfortable position.

As with the bed head and foot parts, the bedside table carcass is also joined with loose flat dowels. The sloping sides represent a construction difficulty: parts (4) to (6) must be bevelled to 10 degrees on the edges bordering the slope. As the table is not itself symmetrical, the second table must, of course, be an exact mirror image of the first.

After cutting to size the carcass parts and cutting mortises for the flat dowels, mark the positions for the drawer mountings. We have chosen specially smooth running drawer runners which are simply screwed to the carcass inner side and correspondingly grooved drawer side.

After that, the parts are glued together. First join the sides to the three bottom shelves. After the glue has set the back is added, again with loose flat dowels.

A construction highlight is the swivel top. For this, a special swivel top bearing is needed. It is fastened with chipboard screws to the top underside, four coach bolts form the connection to the carcass head.

One edge of the bedside table bottom is bevelled by 10 degrees. This is best done using a portable circular saw

Now cut mortises for the flat dowels into the edges. The cutting device attached to an angle grinder is guided along a board clamped to the workpiece by a holdfast

Before gluing the carcass, the drawer mountings should be marked and fixed temporarily. This makes final assembly easier

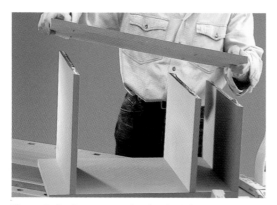

First of all, the carcass is glued without the back. This is fixed − with loose dowels − after the glue has set

Edges and surfaces are thoroughly sanded, then the paint is built up: first a two-pack sealer, then silk finish varnish

The drawer is built in the traditional carpentry manner: Three of the four sides, glued flush together, receive a groove running along the inside into which the bottom is slid underneath the back wall. As one side of each drawer has a 10 degree slope to match the carcass side wall the groove must also be cut at the corresponding angle. To guide the router at this angle, a suitable template must be used.

Now, just the door is missing. It is cut from beech blockboard and fitted to the carcass with two concealed hinges. Finally, the last fittings, the four concealed castors, are screwed on underneath the bottom shelf. With these, the smart bedside table is mobile.

Before revolving top, door and drawer are finally fitted to the carcass, the individual surfaces are treated. As the faces of MDF sheets are very heavily absorbent, it is best to seal first with a two-pack lacquer before the covering paint is applied. Finally, we applied a coat of silk finish clear varnish to all coloured areas and also to the parts made from blockboard. Preferably use environmentally friendly acrylic paint.

Each of the four castors under the bottom shelf is fixed with two coach bolts and two chipboard screws

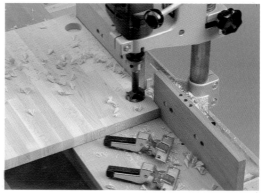

The counter-bored holes for the concealed door hinges are made with a 38 mm cutter

The groove for the drawer bottom must be cut at a 10 degree angle into the sloping side wall

The bearing for the swivel top is first fixed to the top underside and then screwed to the support board

Parts list

No.	Quantity	Name	Dimensions, mm	Material
1	1	Side wall (sloping)	613 × 381	MDF
2	1	Side wall	600 × 381	19 mm
3	1	Front cover	382 × 60	
4	1	Bottom shelf	381 × 371	
5	1	Middle shelf	381 × 304	
6	1	Head board	381 × 279	
7	1	Back	600 × 420	
8	1	Door	359 × 363	19 mm Beech
9	1	Drawer cover	296 × 116	blockboard
10	1	Swivel top	400 × 400	19 mm Beech blockboard

4 castors, Ø 50 mm, 68 mm high; 8 coach bolts M5 × 30 with washers and hexagonal nuts; 2 concealed hinges for doors flush with cabinet, 110 degrees opening; 2 runners; beech drawer carcass: sides 2 × 352 mm long, front and back 266 mm long, each; 1 drawer bottom 5 mm beech plywood, 275 × 344 mm; 2 furniture knobs, Ø 30 mm; 1 swivel bearing (for no. 10); flat dowels; glue

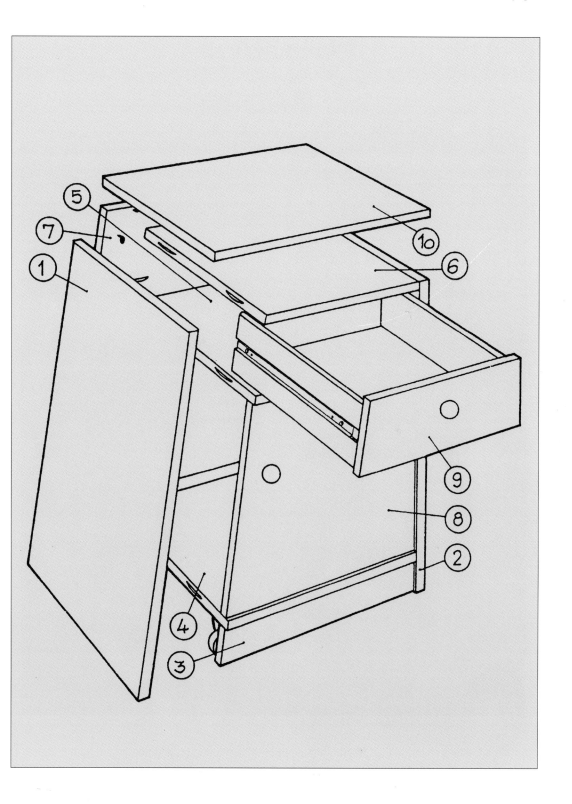

Wall shelves

Do you have a few collector's items which need to be suitably displayed? These beautiful shelves could be the appropriate frame for your favourite ornaments.

Solid furniture made out of pine is most popular. Maybe your home needs additional wall shelves: here they are! We have chosen 28 mm thick pine plywood boards, available at builder's merchants and do-it-yourself stores. In addition you will need a strip, from which the decorative ovolo bead is machined for surrounding the top shelf.

First, the top shelf, bottom and the two shelf ends are cut to size according to the measurements given in the parts list. The next step is to cut the curved lower edges of the shelf ends. Transfer the contours as shown in the drawing onto the wood and then cut with a jigsaw. Use a jigsaw blade for thicker material and switch off the orbiting (pendulum) action. You will achieve a cleaner cut.

Now, cut profiles on both sides of the shelf ends and bottom shelf front edge, using a fine cove cutter. This lessens the heavy appearance of the massive plywood. Use a cutter with guide pin. This is also used along the curved edges. This pin guides along the material edge below the bit and so ensures an exactly constant distance from the edge during cutting.

The individual parts of the shelves are joined with dowels. Mark out on the shelf ends the positions of bottom and top shelf according to the dimensions given on the drawing and then drill four dowel holes for each shelf. Now, put marking pins into the drilled holes and press the side faces of both cross boards against these. In this way, the marking pins transfer the dowel positions onto the edge of the wood, and enable these holes to be drilled. Always drill a few millimetres deeper than the dowel length; this makes it easier to join the pieces and provides a little space for surplus glue. Now, only the strip is missing, which will

The ends are curved by means of a jigsaw. Scribe the cutting line to avoid tearing of the wood

The front edges are profiled with cove cutter. Use offcuts as support to avoid the cutter tilting at the edge

The individual parts are joined with dowels. It is essential to hang the shelf from hooks fitted to the end pieces and not to the top shelf

With aid of the stationary mounted router, the decorative border is made by a series of cuts, using different cutters. Always be sure to move the router from left to right

By treating the surface with linseed oil, the grain is brought out and the wood gets a warm shine

form the upper border. With aid of the stationary mounted router, it is easy to make such a decorative border. Choose a nominal size of 45 × 15 mm, length about 2 m. In our drawing. First an ovolo was used to make a radius at the upper edge. Parallel to the material edge, we continue to work with a cove cutter. After that, we again used an ovolo which created the semicircle rounding. So, after various steps, the profile emerged.

Of course, you may freely use your imagination when cutting ornamental borders. The possibilities are almost unlimited. But never remove too much material at one pass. The least removed, the neater the result. The completed trim is mitre saw cut and then fixed with glue and fine panel pins. Finally, apply linseed oil.

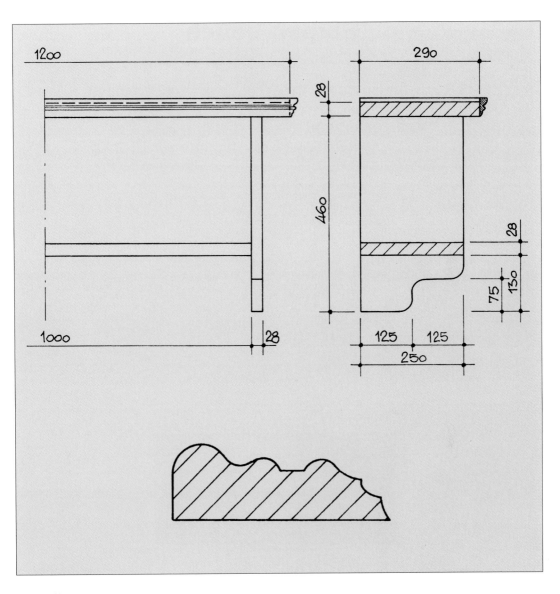

Parts list

Quantity	Name	Dimensions, mm	Material
1	Top shelf	1200 × 290	Pine plywood
1	Bottom shelf	1000 × 250	28 mm thick
2	Shelf ends	460 × 250	

In addition a pine strip 45 × 15 mm, approx. 2 m long for the border; dowels; glue; 2 hooks

Garden bench

During the summer, the balcony and patio enlarge
the living area. Owners of a conservatory may
spend some time all year round amidst their
plants, protected against wind and weather. Our
garden bench offers the ideal resting place

Garden furniture, for long-lasting enjoyment, must be robust and weatherproof. Garden furniture made from plastics are especially popular, as native woods offer only limited resistance against attack from humidity, fungi and bacteria. But after some years, even the best plastics become shabby and brittle. It is only a question of time, when the once smart garden set is taken to the tip.

For the amateur, who builds his own garden furniture, there is a wood which is absolutely weatherproof and especially easy to handle: American red cedar. All over North America, this material is traditionally used for outdoor applications. It has built-in weather protection, which makes it as durable as the precious endangered tropical hardwoods. And the red cedar is also considerably lighter and cheaper. (Environmentally conscious importers guarantee that the wood they sell comes from sustainable forests in Canada.)

We used this material to build a bench in classical English garden furniture style. A comfortable chair results from reducing the width of the seat and back-rest.

Timber yards with a good variety of stock offer American red cedar in planed quality and a variety of dimensions. By using a moisture resistant adhesive, gluing the individual components is not a problem. The dimensions of the required individual parts for the garden bench and chair can be seen in the parts list and drawings (pages 71–73). Following the best traditional methods, mortise-and-tenon joints are used.

First, cut all straight parts with a table circular saw or a fence-guided freehand circular saw. The desired shape for the rearwards leaning back-rests (1) and also the curved cross rails (6) for the seat are

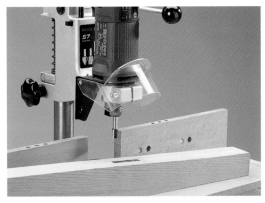

With the stationary mounted router, the groove cutter produces mortises for the construction joint without problem

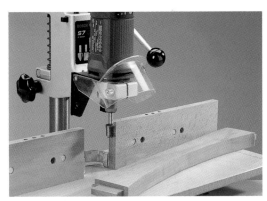

A rebate cutter is used for the tenons. Take a number of shallow cuts, do not overload the tool

Before assembly, the ovolo with guide roller gives smooth radiuses to all material edges

achieved with a bandsaw or circular saw.

When all parts have been prepared, the stationary router with rebate cutter is put into action to cut tenons in the material. (Dimensions to be found in the parts list – see footnote). Material is removed from the end of the workpiece until a 15 mm long tenon remains. Its thickness is roughly ⅓ of the material thickness, i.e. about 10 mm for the long battens (4). Round the edges of each tenon with a rasp. Choose a thickness for which you have the corresponding groove cutter, because you must cut the matching mortise into the receiving part. First, mark out on the workpiece the mortise positions. Then fit the correct straight cutter to the router. The cutter plunges into the wood at the starting point of each mortise, then, the workpiece is moved along the fence until the end is reached. This work is made easier by clamping two auxiliary fences onto the

The boards for the garden bench seats are screwed from underneath to the curved cross beams. Use only stainless steel screws

Two long battens together with the vertical slats form the back rest. Use shims when clamping after gluing to avoid marking the wood. Wipe off surplus glue immediately with a damp cloth

router frame baseplate, between those the piece can then be moved to and fro. It's best to work gradually in several steps until the required depth is reached.

Before assembly, all workpiece edges must be rounded with an ovolo cutter. Then thoroughly sand the wood and fit together the dry parts to check how accurately the parts fit. Finally apply waterproof glue to all joints, before pressing together with cramps. First glue the sides, then insert the assembled back-rest and the front long batten, finally put the seat loose onto the cross battens. Cedar wood does not require surface treatment and may stay outdoors throughout the year without any problem.

If you reduce the width of seat and back-rest according to the dimensions in the parts list, the bench for two will become a garden chair

Parts list

No.	Quantity	Name	Dimensions, mm	Material
1	2	Back supports	900 × 90	Red cedar
2	2	Front supports	565 × 70	42 mm thick
3	2	Arm rests	545 × 70	
4	3	Long battens	1234 (551) long	Red cedar
5	2	Cross battens	440 long	64 × 30 mm
6	2	Cross beam	380 long	Red cedar 48 × 19 mm
7	5	Seat boards	1265 (587) long	Red cedar 66 × 24 mm
8	10 (4)	Back slats	410 long	Red cedar
9	2	Cross battens	440 long	44 × 19 mm

Waterproof glue
Numbers in brackets apply to the chair
For nos. 2 and 3, the length allows for one 15 mm long tenon, each; for nos. 4, 5, 8 and 9, the length allows for two 15 mm long tenons, each

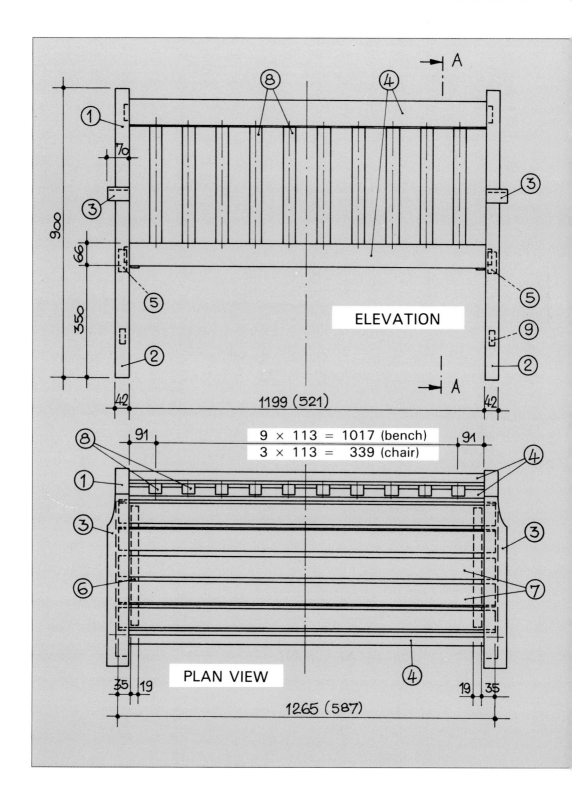

ELEVATION

$9 \times 113 = 1017$ (bench)
$3 \times 113 = 339$ (chair)

PLAN VIEW

1199 (521)

1265 (587)

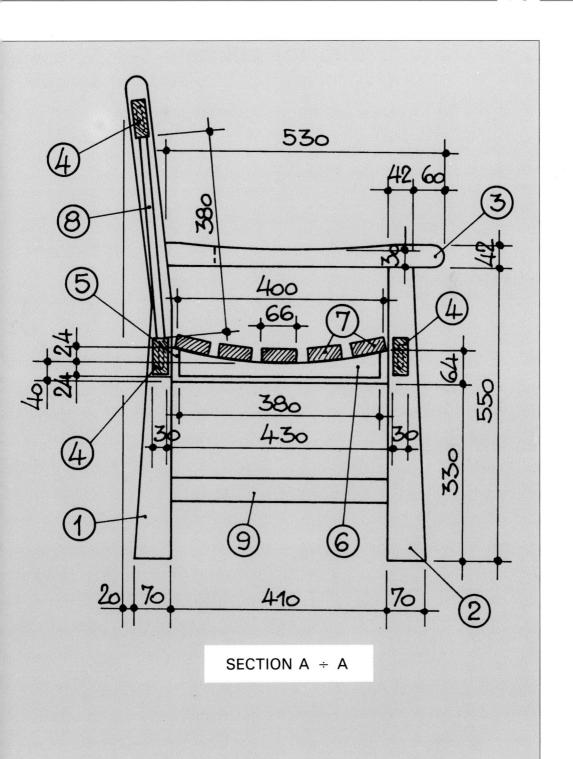

SECTION A ÷ A

Tub for plants

Beautiful plants, on your patio or in the
conservatory are especially attractive if planted in a
tastefully designed tub. Our box design is not only
elegant but also easy to build.

In our country they are guests, who should be looked after so they can grow and flourish: we refer to tub plants from southern climes, which, in these days, can be found on almost every patio. They do need a little bit more than the usual ration of water and occasional plant food. Healthy and strong tub plants are mainly the product of long lasting loving tender care. Only in this way, a little lemon tree or a beautiful long-stem banana plant will become, over the years, a real plant lover's friend. Therefore, what is the most obvious thing to do than to present these precious plants in an appropriate way.

With a router, guided by a straight fence, and using a groove cutter, slots are cut into the posts of the 'fence tub'

Here, we show two, painted and/or stained wood, plant tubs, which elegantly hide the usual unattractive black plastic tubs. With such an 'outfit', the beautiful plant becomes a special eye-catcher on your patio or lovingly arranged conservatory.

In both cases, four posts form the basic structure of the box design. Small palisade fences connect the corner posts of the 'fence tub' arranged in two colours. First, cut the pine posts to size and then bevel the upper ends with four 30 degree cuts. In case you do not own a table circular saw, use carefully a well sharpened handsaw. Before doing this, drill holes at the posts upper ends, which later will take the four pins of the ornamental balls.

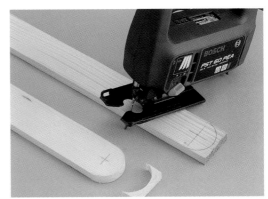

The raised panel slats are easily rounded with a jigsaw and special blade for curves

The next step is to cut the mortise, in which the eight cross bar tenons are set. For this, use a 15 mm groove cutter. The mortises are started 65 mm from the lower edge and are 60 mm long. Distance to the upper mortises is 188 mm. The matching cross bar tenons are 20 mm deep, the mortises should be 2–3 mm deeper to allow some space for surplus glue. The alternating straight and rounded panel slats and also the posts are varnished in a colour of your

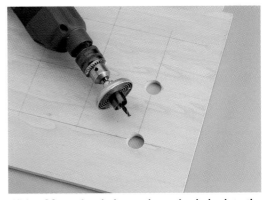

With a 30 mm key hole saw bore nine holes into the tub bottom, for draining surplus water

The posts of the white tub have a 6 mm groove to take the side panels. Use the router with a straight fence

Mark an arc on the upper ends of the posts and round correspondingly with a rasp, followed by careful sanding

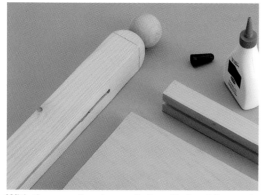

With the use of waterproof glue, fit the side panels of the white tub into the grooves of the posts

choice and, using a waterproof glue, screwed together with the cross bars from inside. Fix the carriers to the four lower cross bars for the tub bottom to rest on. The plywood sheet receives nine 30 mm holes, which take care of draining surplus water. Finally, all parts get again a coat of waterproof varnish.

Four pine posts, 45 × 45 mm and 500 mm long, are required to build the white plant tub. Cut the posts to size; mark the diagonals at the upper end of each post, their intersection will mark the middle, where the dowel holes for the ornamental balls are drilled.

Draw onto each side of each post the longitudinal centre line, mark its midpoint. Draw an arc (of radius half the post length!) around this point upwards. This will give you the shape for rounding the upper end. Remove with a rasp, at each of the four post sides, the material above the arcs, until the post is accurately round.

Now cut the eight rails and also the four side panels. Fit a 6 mm straight cutter into the router and cut downwards in the centre of the posts and the rails a 10 mm deep groove. At the top, the rails are 50 mm below the post ends, at the bottom 20 mm. Assembly and gluing is done in two steps. First fit together with glue (waterproof) the rails and the side panels. At the sides, the plywood must jut out 10 cm. Apply glue to the post grooves and insert this projection. The large glue line of the joint allows flat fitting of the rails.

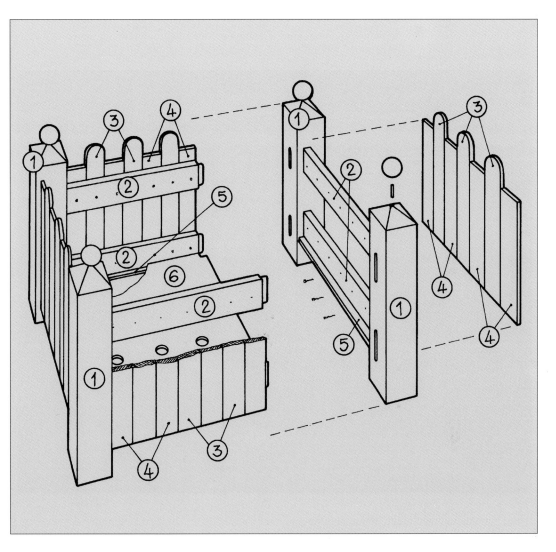

Parts list

No.	Quantity	Name	Dimensions, mm	Material
1	4	Posts	480 long	Pine, 70 × 70 mm
2	8	Cross bars	390 long	Pine, 70 × 20 mm
3	12	Panel slats	420 long	Pine, 50 × 12 mm
4	16	Panel slats	370 long	
5	4	Carriers	345 long	Pine, 35 × 10 mm
6	1	Tub bottom	388 × 388	Plywood, 10 mm
4 wooden balls, 50 mm diameter; 4 wooden dowels 6 mm diameter × 70 mm; chipboard screws, waterproof glue				

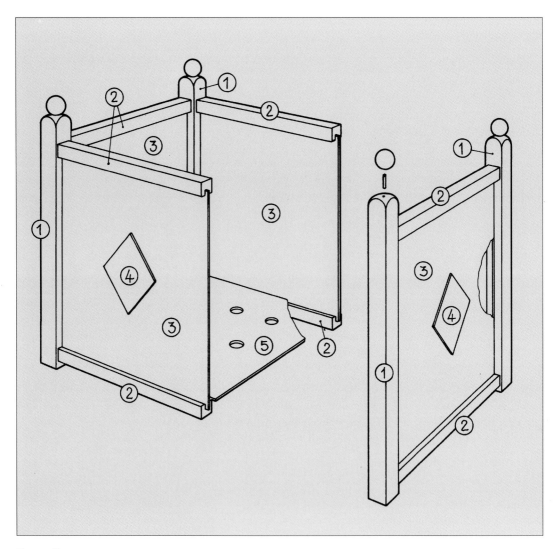

Parts list

No.	Quantity	Name	Dimensions, mm	Material
1	4	Posts	500 long	Pine, 45 × 45 mm
2	8	Rails	350 long	Pine, 35 × 30 mm
3	4	Side panels	390 × 370	Plywood
4	4	Decoration	160 × 120	6 mm thick
5	1	Tub bottom	387 × 387	Plywood, 10 mm
4 wooden balls 45 mm diameter; 4 wood dowels 6 mm diameter × 60 mm, waterproof glue				

Index

First published in Germany in 1994 by Falken-Verlag GmbH,
65527 Niedernhausen/Ts

First published in Great Britain by Argus Books 1994

Argus Books
Argus House
Boundary Way
Hemel Hempstead
Herts HP2 7ST
England

© 1994 by Falken-Verlag GmbH

Translated by Irmtraud Hare

ISBN 1-85486-111-5

Cover photograph by the author
Photographs: author's archive; archive of Deutsche
              Heimwerker Akademie; editors of *Selbst ist der
              Mann* (design proposal double bed and
              bedside table)
Illustrations: Jürgen Reinbold, Mechernich

Typeset by The Studio, Exeter
Printed and bound in Hong Kong by the Paramount Printing Group